Love more. Fear less.
Float more. Steer less.

Essays by John Halcyon Styn

About this book:

This collection is a work in progress - as is life.
Any similarities to actual people, events, or miracles are far from coincidental.

For Grandpa Caleb & all Love Warriors.

Contents:

Letter to Remind Myself Who I Want To Be Today

Good morning and welcome to this brand new day!

Your existence today is a miracle – every thought, sight, and sensation is a gift.

You are an expression of the divine.

You will attend to daily tasks, but never forget that your purpose is to show and share Love.

You are a blessing on the world.

Your smile and warm eyes are gifts you can share all day long.

You can see the divine seed in everyone. And you feel compassion for all.

You are unaffected by others' stress and anger.

You are connected to all things.

You have the ability to be in harmony with everyone and everything.

You refuse to retaliate or be lured into conflict.

You are confident, but humble.

You are a good listener.

You are open to possibility.

You pay attention to roadside flowers, cloud formations, and children's faces.

You see the miracles present in every moment.

You are overflowing with gratitude.

You will never have this day again… Enjoy!

Life is Art

"I am a Lifestyle artist."

I've had that phrase atop my personal websites and business cards for many years.

Once in a while, someone asks me, "What the heck does that mean?"

To me, it comes down to the question of "What is Art?" And, "What is an Artist?"

We are socialized to see Art as something that occurs within very specific borders with very specific mediums.

When we are young, we have specific arts and crafts time. But when we grow up, "making art" is about as socially acceptable as "eating paste."

Art becomes something that exists in rectangular frames and is hung on walls.

But a painting on the wall is no different than an aquarium in your living room. It may be a tiny taste of the ocean... but it is NOT the sea!

We fall victim to snooty judgments of good and bad art that is defined by trends and academic concepts WAY outside our personal perceptions.

Art becomes something that has such specific definitions that most people adorn their walls with re-prints of famous paintings. It is much easier to hang a well established "Art" print than navigate the esoteric art world and risk having your choices ridiculed.

But art is not defined by its materials or the tools used to create it. Art is not defined by whether or not it gets hung on a gallery wall.

This is another travesty of modern socialization: There is little room for art in a capitalist system. We see art as a luxury item that is put in a display case. But I would argue it is more like a philosophy.

Art is a way of seeing your surroundings.

Art is a way of not taking things for granted.

Art is a way to see the WORLD as a stage.

A Gallery is to Art as a Zoo is to the Animal Kingdom.

It is just a pinhole glimpse! (That is not to say that galleries or zoos cannot be awesome.) But to believe that the Gallery is the beginning and end of Art is to live life with the dullest of blinders.

Art is working to see the worn grooves of socialized patterns and ask, "Why?"

Art is questioning the definitions of beauty or mundane and striving to actually SEE the world.

Art is an attempt to clear out all the definitions, judgments, values, and fears that have been layered upon you your entire life. It is the process of trying to open up to a creative force that is ever-present in you – but deeply buried. It is an attempt to "get clear" and allow this divine creative force to flow THROUGH you. To allow yourself to be a tool of the universe. To speak, write, draw, paint, dance, think, and see unencumbered by your ego and socialization.

To be an artist is to be on a quest to "get clear."

So to be a Lifestyle Artist is to see every step as an act of creative expression -- To attempt to allow every movement and every choice to be driven by that inner divine flow.

When great art is created, it is channeled through the artist. We can shower praise on that person, but his real feat is getting out of the way and ALLOWING the creative expression to flow through him. *(The artist is still deserving of praise as this IS an impressive feat.)*

Art is the miraculous that is ever-present.

And being an Artist is as simple as seeking the miraculous in ourselves and allowing it to come forth.

A Lifestyle Artist is simply one who strives to allow the creative flow to instruct every aspect of his life. This path doesn't look any specific way – it is simply the result of a way of seeing.

And when the entire world is a canvas – it is impossible to color outside the lines. There is no good art and bad art. There is only personal truth.

Now go eat some paste and let yourself see.

Sabotage Re-write

I have been sabotaging my own story.

I have been telling people that I am self-employed and that I have hired myself to write. This has actually been a good way for me to look at it as I am motivated to write every morning and come to it with a sense of pride and duty.

But I have been quick to follow up with, "I was fortunate enough to put away some savings, so I have a window where I have the luxury of not having to work. When my money runs out, I'm not sure what I'll do. But I'm enjoying it while I can!"

This felt like an intelligent, responsible part of my story. But I realized it is totally based on fear.

I am afraid of people reacting negatively to my freedom.

I feel embarrassed for not having more struggle in my life right now, so I put this, "Oh, but it is temporary!" caveat at the end.

It's like I'm waiting for the other shoe to drop.

WTF?

This goes against everything else I've been experiencing lately. ALL the evidence I'm collecting reinforces the belief that if I stay in integrity and trust the Flow, I will be rewarded.

So why am I afraid to believe the same thing about financial abundance?

I have been consciously and actively trying to "Float more, steer less." And the places the current has directed me have been beyond belief. There is no logical reason why I wouldn't surrender my future finances in the same way.

A friend recently said boldly, "Oh, I don't worry about money. I'm always given ways to get what I need."

My first reaction was, "How naïve." But then I realized... this was true for me as well! My fears about being broke have always been far worse than any reality. And yet, I somehow have developed the beliefs that being financially optimistic was a form of stupidity.

I also had a momentary reaction of "Sure, I bet some rich dude saves you when your bank account gets low."

Ewww! What a petty, judgmental thought! I dismissed it as soon as it crossed my mind. But it shined a bright light on some self-judgments I was unaware of.

And it was these self-judgments that were making me sabotage my story.

I'd hate people to think I had it too easy or resent me for being overly lucky.

Deep down I know that I have worked hard to shift my thoughts and life to the place it is in now, but my unhealthy beliefs on the surface are strong.

Jacob Glass told a story in a recent lecture where a friend said to him, "So you hang out all week, chilling in coffee shops reading and writing. Then once a week you work a few hours and give a lecture?! Must be nice!!!"

To which Jacob's response was, "It's FUCKING AWESOME! And there is plenty of room."

I have been so afraid that someone will say, "Must be nice!" that I have removed the happy ending from my own story.

That chapter is over. Here is the re-write:

"I *am* a writer.

I am working on a book, a weekly podcast, an iphone app, a charity effort, a Burning Man camp, and all sorts of other projects in varying stages.

I am dedicated to loving more, and fearing less. To floating more, and steering less.

My needs are always met.

And it's fucking awesome."

I was told to get some experience before applying to grad schools. So, after college graduation, I got one of the few jobs available in Psychology for someone without a grad degree: I worked as a counselor in a locked down group home for boys 6-12.

On my first day, I got chased around the property by a kid wildly swinging a garden rake. Later that day I was spit on.

After 18 months working in the group home, I was miserable. I was living with my parents and dreaded going to work. I wore my long hair in a bun on the top of my hair to avoid getting it pulled during restraints. *("Restraints" = physically subduing a violent child according to a specific training. What a terrible thing that was.)*

It is no wonder that after 18 months at the facility, I was considered an old-timer. Very few counselors lasted past 2 years. The job had few rewards.

It gave me an insane amount of respect for co-workers and social workers who had been doing it for years. Day after day, they go to the dark corners of society and try to help.

At the Group Home I saw clearly that activism can go in 2 directions: 1) Attacking problems or 2) Changing environments that cause problems – Fighting Dark vs. Spreading Light.

Both are helpful.

In the early days of Hug Nation, I received my share of criticism – "If you want to really help people, go work in a soup kitchen!"

But that seems narrow minded, to me. Help is needed in many ways. It would be short sighted to think that dark fighting is always more urgent.

It would be like telling someone who is building a long term irrigation system that if they really wanted to help the farmer, they would get down and do some weeding. Sure, the weeding is needed, but an irrigation system can change the very nature of the landscape.

That being said, after my 2 years in the group home, I focused almost exclusively on Light Spreading efforts. The darkness of the group home had taken its toll on me.

The Course in Miracles talks about "effortless charity" – meaning that you can dedicate your energy to helping without it feeling like a sacrifice. For me, I had only experienced this with detached "Light Spreading" efforts like Hug Nation. I associated Dark Fighting with screaming kids, being spit in the face, and just generally going to a depressing headspace.

I have desires to help, but not at the expense of my own joy. This may sound like a selfish statement, but I no longer think so. It does no good to join someone in their suffering. If someone was tumbling down a raging river, would it make sense to jump in and try to save them? Then you would both be cold and wet. And you'd not be in much of a position to help at all.

But if you could stay dry, calm, and optimistic – you could figure out what resources are available to lift the other person up without dragging you down. Further, while not an immediate solution, working on teaching swim classes and water safety could help provide a long term solution to improve the situation in the future.

It is reminiscent of the old adage, "Give a man a fish and he eats for a day. Teach him to fish and he eats for a lifetime."

But a couple weekends ago I had an epiphany about charity. After spending all day joyfully helping people I love, I realized that there are tons of ways of helping people that do not feel like "Dark Fighting" at all.

It is possible to give of yourself without feeling depleted. It doesn't have to feel like a sacrifice at all. In fact, it could even make you feel so good that your motivation **feels** like it is selfish.

This was a huge perspective shift for me: To realize that service does not have to be sacrifice – Giving time and energy can be a joyful, loving act.

There is an interview with my grandfather that I have watched dozens of times, He looks into the camera and says, "At this point in my life it is clear to me that I should dedicate whatever time I have left to loving people…and helping people."

I think I finally understand.

Selfish Faith

I used to believe deeply that the world was messed up and needed fixing.

But as I learned and read and grew, I recognized that nobody is in possession of the blueprint. No human can decide what *fixed* looks like.

Hitler had a vision of Utopia. So did the Pharaohs. So did every tyrant. I'm sure their committee meetings were filled with congratulatory back-patting.

How are we to know that our Master Plan is righteous?

We can't.

I let go of the idea that the external world is something that I can fix.

Or that I could even have the perspective to know what "fixing" looked like.

Instead I turned inward.

I embraced Faith.

Not "Faith" in a higher power. But Faith that my only battle ground is my own mind and heart. Faith that if I heal my mind and embrace Love – then I will affect the world as I am meant to.

This can appear quite selfish.

And it often feels selfish, too.

But I had Faith.

If I follow my heart and pursue Love, then I AM playing my part in the Master Plan. The destination is not my responsibility.

I am but one cell in a massive organism. And my role is to discover my true self and walk my walk.

A white blood cell does not need to know that the body is climbing a mountain. It only needs to know that the foreign microbe in front of it needs to be dealt with.

Each cell need only to stay pure and walk it's walk. In fact, to become more ambitious than this or believe that they "know" the master plan is the very definition of sickness. A cancerous cell forgets that it has a single role in a massive system and instead tries to enact it's own selfish plan on the rest of the body.

I'm sure the cancer believes it is heroic.

And I'm sure every missionary believes he is righteous.

There is a wonderful quote at the beginning of the film, "HERO" that says, *"In any war, there are heroes on both sides."*

That is because both sides, in fact all "sides," are driven by external beliefs. Inner truth and our own individual paths are all we can know for certain.

In a world swirling with judgment and accepted belief systems, this type of inward trust requires Faith.

So as I work to free myself of shame, I have faith.

As I confront my own fears, I have faith.

Faith that the person underneath all my socialization is a perfect seed of the divine.

Faith that when I can act from that pure self, I am acting as an agent of Love.

Faith that self-growth can be a more significant activism than any external act.

Do I question my Faith? Hell yes! I stumble daily.

But with each week, I gain more confidence.

With each chapter, I gather more evidence.

Our Life is our Purpose. Our daily walk is our Service.

And EVERYTHING we do can be infused with Love.

My recent involvement with the monthly "Help The Homeless" has been one of the strongest affirmations of my Faith to date.

Not because of the physical manifestation of any specific action, but because of the way the inspiration grew in me.

I did not set out to do a good deed.

I had a realization one day that: Helping people I love brought me deep Joy.

This was transformative. Helping people was always something I did in an effort to be nice. To keep the balance between friends. To pull my weight.

But as I studied and learned and grew, I turned a corner.

I think it had much to do with the awareness of Connection.

If we are all connected, then your Joy brings me Joy.

If we are all one, then your gain is my gain.

If I give to you, I am giving to me. There is nothing saintly about it… it is selfish pleasure.

Not only that, but if you can derive pleasure from what happens to OTHERS, that means the entire world is an opportunity for Joy.

I'll say that again: **"The entire world is an opportunity for Joy."**

NOT because of what they can give me. But because if what I can give them. If I can raise "them" then I raise myself.

This seemed so abstract…but not after Valentine's Day 2010.

Jason called from the Costco Parking Lot. "I just bought a crap-load of stuff for the homeless. Want to come with me to pass it out?"

It was not something I would have done myself. I had never visited "Skid Row" and had fear on several levels. But with the recent epiphanies about Gifting and Joy, his invitation seemed divinely inspired.

We drove downtown in the Hugmobile and hoped for the best.

It was chaotic, it was fast, it was amazing. When all the goodies had been given away we both had huge smiles and couldn't wait to do it again.

I am 38 years old and had never done something like that.

And to be honest, I don't think I was ready to until now. Sure, I could have handed out granola bars and fed bellies for the day. But it was the awareness of connection that made the experience so rewarding. This time I was not doing my "duty" or easing any guilt. I was acting selfishly – feeling pleasure at the increase in Love and Connection.

My Faith was rewarded.

A month later we did it again. More people joined us and donated.

This weekend was the next "First Saturday" and we did it again. Even more people participated.

I wish I could take credit for some grand vision or Master Plan.

But this rippling of goodness was not the result of anyone "making things happen." There was no agenda or desired outcome. Everything was the result of people following their hearts and acting from a place of Love.

The outcome is always unknown, but my Faith in this "selfish" path continues to grow.

Ed. Note: This seed has become 1stSaturdays.org and continues to grow.

What's The Story?

In describing my recent experiences with visiting the homeless, I mentioned that I do not join people in their story.

I got an email asking for some clarification: *"Isn't empathy for your fellow man one of the highest forms of humanity?"*

Yes, and no.

I think we can have empathy for conditions, without believing the story.

A story may be factually accurate, but told through a filter of negativity. Too often we use our stories as prisons. The way we see and interpret our lives (i.e. the way we tell our story) makes all the difference in the world.

"I am shy."

"I never have luck with women."

"The government is screwing me."

A negative story does nothing for us in the present moment except anchor us to a path we do not want.

I try to resist judgment, good or bad, of someone's condition. Who am I to know that having a 5 year plan is better than being lost? Or that working a 9-5 is better than being homeless?

I know what story our culture teaches us. But our culture is full of anger, depression, and mindless drudgery. I hardly think "culture" is a trusted source.

Which is why it is important to not buy in to the status quo story and be a part of the forces that re-enforce someone's victim role, anger, or helplessness.

When we visit a homeless person, we need to let go of the story.

This is a person in front of me. Not a homeless person.

This is a person who currently does not have resources. Not a victim screwed by the system and followed by bad luck.

There is no value in re-enforcing and re-telling a story that we don't enjoy.

The reality is that many of us LOVE to re-tell our upsetting stories. We feel comfortable in the victim role. We love the feeling of righteous indignation as we complain.

People can stay in those stories if they like. But I refuse to join them.

You may argue for your limitations, but I don't have to agree.

I believe we are all perfect. We all have the potential for Joy.

And I certainly am in no position to know if your situation is bad or good.

All I know to be true in this moment is that I have a granola bar and you are hungry.

In that moment we are not the sum of all our stories. We are simply present with one another. We are two expressions of divine consciousness in human form. Dragging all my past upsets into this moment would not honor the past – it would dirty the present.

Now, this isn't to say I refuse to believe someone is feeling sadness, hurt, pain, etc.. The feelings are real and we should honor them. But when the story is contributing to those unpleasant feelings, there is no reason to hold on to it so tightly.

Stories can be ladders, but they usually are prisons. If it doesn't lift you up, then let it go.

Life Isn't Fair.

Life isn't fair.

That is one of the first things I remember learning from my folks.

When I would painfully scream about the size of my ice cream serving compared to my brother's, they would calmly respond. *"Life isn't fair."*

It seemed cold and unfeeling at the time.

But now I see how important that awareness is.

First off, it is true.

There is no line judge for the Game of Life. There is no umpire to blow a whistle when someone gets an unfair advantage.

It is just the reality. Before a child is born, the circumstances of their parents already play a massive role in the opportunities and challenges that await that child. A child born in Somalia will simply not have the same opportunities as one born in Santa Monica. My grandpa used to call this the "Obstetrical Accident" that determines the country and social-economic class of our birth. (Some would argue that this is no accident at all – but just a logical result of karmic cycles. More on that later.)

Some cultures have legal systems that try to soften the most obscene of the inequalities, but they are surface fixes to much deeper issues. Just because opportunities are equal under the law, doesn't mean that things are fair.

Compared to 50 years ago, cultural discrimination around the world (in most situations) has improved. But even though the inequality heals more every day, even a fully healed culture will have the scars of old beliefs forever.

But the truth is that EVERYONE has their own specific set of gifts as well as obstacles. Even siblings growing up under the same roof can have vastly different opportunities. In many cultures, just being born second, or female, can make all the difference in the world.

It is not fair.

And that doesn't even touch upon the incredibly unfair biology that is handed out person to person. Some are faster, some are smarter. Some are faster, smarter, stronger, AND were born into economic wealth.

None of it is fair.

While there is no denying that certain circumstances create more obstacles, it is important to remember that getting an unfair advantage is not necessarily a good thing.

In an old South park episode, they show the debilitating effects that being unfairly good looking can have on your personality. When everyone laughs at your jokes and agrees with you because they have a crush on you, it creates a skewed sense of self and warped understanding of the world. The path of the pretty person may be easier, but that doesn't mean it leads to good things.

Often it takes adversity to awaken the truly wonderful things inside us.

When scientists set up the BioDome project, they tried to create a fully enclosed environment – with plants, water, and animals all isolated and contained under a massive dome. After a period of time, the tallest trees starting falling over and scientists were stumped. There were no diseases or problems that they could see. The researchers eventually figured out that the trees, even with all the sun and water they required – did not develop properly in the bubble. Without the blowing wind, the trees' root structures did not grow deep and strong. Without the daily "struggles" of gusts and storms, the tree did not develop the necessarily support system to support the adult tree.

People, just like trees, **need** obstacles to build their strength. And actually, from this perspective, one can shift his view of obstacles themselves. If a challenge is required for growth, then it isn't an obstacle at all – but a classroom and stepping stone.

From this perspective is it more "unfair" to have an easy childhood? Or a challenge-filled one?

It quickly becomes clear that – like so much in life – we are in no position to judge.

All we can do is work with what we've got. And do the best we can.

It can be tempting to feel sorry for people with fewer advantages. Don't do it!

We have no vantage point to know what anyone's life is supposed to look like – including our own. Think of a great person you consider a hero. Would they have become the person they did with a different life story?

Sometimes when I am overwhelmed with a struggle in my life I try to visualize my life as a book. What kind of book would I want my life to be? Would I want to be a boring tale with minimal conflict? Or a grand epic with massive highs and lows?

Another tendency is to feel guilty for the unfair blessings in your life. If you slip into this perspective, try to replace that feeling with gratitude immediately. Imagine if you gave someone a gift and they say, "oh! No, you shouldn't! It's too much! Take it back!" It would rob you of the joy of giving the gift.

Instead learn to receive joyfully and simply acknowledge your gratitude. Instead of feeling bad and trying to dismiss the gift, feel good and exalt it. When you embrace a gift, it energizes you and gives you the resources to "pay it forward." Imagine that all your advantages AND challenges are prerequisites for the role you play in the Universe – whatever that may be. Feeling guilty for the gifts of your birth would be like a bird feeling guilty for it's song.

If you feel disadvantaged – imagine all your struggles as a cosmic classroom.

If you feel over-privileged – imagine your resources as tools of the Universe.

Life isn't fair.

Thank God.

The Secret

One of the big problems with "The Secret" is that it promises people that they can get what they want.

But what people want is Porches, Palaces, and 6-packs.

Those things are what we picture in our dreams or post on our vision boards.

But we loose track of the idea that the reason we want those things is because of the feeling we associate with it: Affluence, Comfort, Health, etc..

The reality is things rarely bring the feeling we associate with them. At least, not for very long. Sure, there is a thrill when we get a new toy. But that thrill fades.

When Byron Katie was asked about The Secret, she said it teaches you to get what you want, "I teach you how to want what you have."

And this distinction regarding goals highlights the difference between traditional and spiritual schools of thought.

Traditional thinking believes, "I'll be content as soon as I reach this goal." It could be a promotion, a degree, a body fat percentage, a girlfriend, or a clean bill of health.

The spiritual thinker asks, "How can I be content with things exactly as they are?"

The first group strives to change the exterior circumstances of the world to meet their goals.

The second strives to change the way they think about the exterior circumstances.

The first group thinks the second group is lazy and lacks ambition.

The second group thinks the first group is chasing a carrot on a stick.

There is a wonderful Zen story about a monk who sets out from the monastery to explore the world. But as he begins to walk, his feet get pricked and cut on the rough ground. Tired of the pain, he sets out to cover the ground in front of him with leather in order to protect his feet.

At which point the master offers the advice, "Why not simply wrap the leather around your feet?"

The only thing we ever have control over is ourselves. So it is a fool's game to try to change the world in order to make us content. Far more rational is to learn how to wrap our feet in leather. How can we adjust our minds so that the exterior world – no matter what thorns or sharp rocks it contains – remains something we can appreciate and enjoy.

And this is the major flaw in "The Secret." The law of attraction is indeed a powerful tool. But unless we work on our own minds, we fail to know how to use it. We pave the world with leather, thinking that our naïve solution is best.

When we can learn to surrender to the reality of the world as it is, we can see the ever-present gifts around us… and the miracles in every moment.

Wealth

I am learning that there are a whole lotta ways to be rich.

For years I always associated "wealth" with financial riches. But my thinking has changed.

First of all, money is just a symbol.

When it became too difficult to trade corn directly for apples, a system of symbolic worth was established.

This symbolic token is worth 1 bushel of corn or it's agreed upon equivalent (2 bags of apples, 3 hours labor painting a house, 4 grams of spices, etc..)

I think this is an important reminder: Money can only matter in context of what it symbolizes to you.

I say, "to you" because people project all sorts of meaning onto their bank accounts. For example, many people associate money with a feeling of security. This is absurd.

There is no such thing as real security. A huge bank account will not protect you from health problems, aging, accidents, or heartache.

At best, it can remove the stress of how you will attain food and shelter. But even that "security" is dependent on a stable financial and social system.

I don't mean to knock money. It is awesome!

It can buy you nice things. And allows you to pay people to do things for you (and therefore buy you Time.)

But this illustrates my initial point: There are many ways to be rich.

Being "Time Affluent" is one of those ways.

Having a rich social life, or being abundantly healthy are others.

If you are sacrificing your time, relationships, or health in order to be "money rich," then you are simply choosing one type of affluence over another.

And, since money is only a symbolic token, it does very little for you when you don't trade it for wealth in those other areas.

For example, I am currently trading my accrued financial resources for time affluence. (AKA "living off my savings.")

This makes me "time rich" – and I love it. I am writing, growing relationships, and connecting with my community. I've learned that time and freedom are far more valuable to me than property or cars.

In fact, it makes me analyze my life even further. How much more could I simplify? Before my savings runs out, what else could I exchange for time? Do I need such a nice place to live? Would a new camera really affect my ability to produce art?

I am staying open to financial affluence, but not at the expense of my other realms.

The exciting thing about opening up the definition of wealth is that it allows infinite opportunities for "success."

Traditionally, "success" has a very limited definition that is mostly dependent on financial riches. And the cultural image of wealth has a pretty rigid definition. But when the awareness of wealth and riches are expanded, awesome futures can take any form! Many of us have been struggling to color inside the lines, without realizing there are many more ways to evaluate a picture. (Vividness of color, creativity, etc..) We may be rich already and not even be aware.

Make sure you don't get so focused on your bank balance that you forget your life balance. In the end, our internal state of happiness is the only measuring stick.

Attached to Outcome

There are two huge consequences to staying attached to outcome.

The first is that we feel intense frustration.

Frustration is caused by one thing: Wishing things were different than they are.

We tend to feel this frustration regardless of how much control we have over the situation. In situations where we have no control, the ridiculousness of attachment is easy to see.

Imagine a rainy day and you are stuck in traffic. (Just visualizing it makes my gut tense up.)

There are two places our thoughts can go: 1) Accept the reality of the situation. Or, 2) Wish it was different.

The physical situation does not change based on which place your thoughts go. Your commute is slowed, regardless. In both cases, you will have 45 minutes in your car. But the way you experience those 45 minutes can vary drastically.

And that experience is wholly dependent on your thoughts.

When we wish things were different, it is because we are holding on to our expectations for the experience – even as Reality demonstrates something quite different.

We planned on being home 10 minutes ago. Now we will miss the beginning of our favorite TV show and our family will have to wait to start dinner. Our kids will get restless which will then cause our spouse more hardships.

It is easy to collect imaginary evidence of the injustice.

But it is important to recognize that these hardships are all imagined. You are comparing the Reality of the present moment to a fictional story you have in your head of how it "should" be. The fact that you are sitting and listening to your car stereo isn't frustrating. What frustrates you is that you planned for something different. When we are unable to let go of our attachment to that outcome, all we can see is what went wrong.

One possible reaction to this awareness would be to stop making plans entirely. Someone recently told me that their mantra was "Expectation kills the joy."

But the key is not to be without plans. The key is to be unattached to plans working out exactly as you imagined them.

The second consequence to being attached to outcome is that we become blind to whatever gifts and experiences the world provides for us, because we are not looking for them.

Lets return to the traffic situation. Suppose instead of wanting to be home by 6:30, you shifted your goal to, "I want to have quality time with my family after work." Because isn't that really what you want? We create a specific plan to attain that goal, but when we stay overly attached to that plan, it is easy to fail.

The second, more vague, "plan" could work out in an infinite number of ways, whereas the "home by 6:30" plan was a frustrating failure the minute the roads got wet with rain.

With a less specific, unattached, goal, you can allow the present moment to be what it is AND allow the unknown future to still satisfy your aims.

Regardless of what time you get home, you can still have a wonderful experience with your family. In fact, I would argue that coming home frustrated from the drive and spending a full hour in a pissy mood would be much worse than coming home with a peaceful headspace and having a fraction of the time.

This is why it is important to seek things like, "a feeling of abundance" instead of "A Porche."

It is ridiculous how confident we often are in our own plans – especially when life experience shows us time and time again that we are naïve.

How many times have you thought during transition, "Please God, don't let them leave / help me keep this job / fix this situation for me!"

But when you look back years later have thought, "Thank GOD I'm not still with that person / at that job / down that path!"

"The Course in Miracles" teaches that we are in no position to know if we are in advance or retreat.

Reminding yourself that you often do not know what your best interests are can be a helpful tool in letting go of attachment.

There is an old saying that "When God shuts a door, he opens a window." Unfortunately, if you exhaust yourself trying to pry open the closed door, you won't ever see the window. Opportunity will be missed if your tunnel vision stays attached to an outcome no longer available.

So next time you are "stuck" in your car, try to be critical of your thoughts. With an unknown about of time to sit, how will you spend those minutes?

You can stay stuck in a loop of "Things should be different!" Or you can look for the opportunities present in the reality. Maybe you focus on the music on your radio. Maybe you call an old friend. Maybe you spend some time thinking about and planning an outing for your family. Or maybe you just re-play happy memories in your head.

Will you fight the tide or ride the waves?

You will arrive home at the exact same time.

I am enjoying a time affluence right now. I have lots of free time to write, to visit friends, to do whatever I want. It is glorious.

I am living off my savings. But since my savings are finite, this is only a temporary lifestyle.

I love not having to hustle for clients or help corporations make more sales.

It is the ageless challenge: How do I get enough resources to live comfortably with a job/plan/income that I am also comfortable with?

I have really been enjoying the "Float more" luxury of time abundance. It is such a nice feeling that I find myself thinking, "How cheaply could I live?" How deep a sacrifice could I make? Could I simplify my life into a laptop and motor home? Become a digital monastic nomad? What about moving to a country where my savings would last longer?

It is all abstract right now, but the idea of returning to a 9-5 desk job sounds like an unendurable torture. What possible ways could I make it work? I would so much rather strip away things from my life than give up time to have them. At some point I'll have to make some hard choices.

Even though I have already designated this time as one where I will not be getting income, I find it hard to relax. I need to routinely return to the mental statement that I am "on Plan."

This period of time is not intended to be a vacation. When my last client contract ended, I did not view it as unemployment. I am thinking of this period as one of SELF employment. In some ways it is like going back to school. I am focused on writing, breaking web surfing habits, getting clear, and being open to direction from the Universe. My own half-assed Walden Pond.

And so far, I have been thrilled with the growth my mind and spirit have demonstrated. I have no idea where it is headed, but I have Faith that a solution will come to me.

I need to keep returning to this mantra, "I have Faith."

It is a type of Faith I'm still wrapping my head around. It is a faith in the tools and truths that I've gathered up til now and continue to learn.

Faith in the power of Now.

Faith in the interconnectedness of all things.

Faith in non-attachment.

And Faith that if I embrace these things and focus on Love, then the natural flow of the universe is for me to live harmoniously and happy.

This Faith is what dissolves the stories that cause the fear.

It is not a concrete process. It can not be solidified with logical argument. There is not a math equation that balances out nicely.

When we create plans for ourselves, we depend on these logical stories. "I'll get my degree, then I'll be able to get a better job, then I'll get that thing I want." Makes perfect sense.

But the problem with a plan like that is that, with a "correct" outcome, it means that there are an infinite number of ways of things going WRONG. That makes any bump in the road into a stressful thing.

This is the gift of non-attachment. If you are not attached to the outcome, you are able to see the opportunity in every obstacle. Flunking out of school is not a failure, but a whole new realm of possibilities. Breaking a leg is not a hindrance to your marathon plans, but divine enrollment in a new course of reading study.

It is more than just looking for the silver lining. It is letting go of your plan so that you can see and appreciate the lining, even if it is gold.

Bottom line: My Now is wonderful and jam-packed with possibility. The only "wrong" path would be to lose sight of my blessings or get so concerned with the future that the present passes me by without me in it.

I just need to return to Faith.

It is easy to slip into the mentality that we are powerless over our feelings. If things go well for us, we feel happy. If things work out poorly, we feel unhappy.

But Happiness is not the simple result of our circumstances.

Happiness is actually more of a tool – in the same way that "pain" is a tool. Pain helps let us know the degree in which we are physically damaging the body.

Happiness helps let us know the state of our thoughts.

Think of our state of Happiness as a sophisticated monitoring system. It's like our own personal "Google Analytics" – if we only knew how to read the tools.

We tend to think that we are happy when things are going well for us, and frustrated when the world is not going our way. But this is only partially true.

Our level of happiness does not reflect the state of our world, but the state of our thoughts.

It is like looking at the "temperature" dial on your car and believing that the needle moves depending on how hard you are driving the vehicle. In reality, it is the condition of the engine – the oil level & the efficiency of the cooling system – that plays a much more important role. Even a car standing still at a low idle will overheat if the engine is not healthy. Conversely, a well-maintained engine will keep the temperature smack in the "normal" zone, regardless of how fast you drive, and no matter how many hills you climb.

Can you avoid big hills to avoid car strain? Absolutely!

According to the metaphor, this would be the process of removing toxic elements from your life.

• Are there people in your life that are negative or judgmental? Do you feel worse about yourself or the world after spending time with them?

• Do you attend social gatherings that cause you anxiety? Do you feel drained and defeated afterwards?

• Do you consume alarmist news or entertainment? Does it leave you feeling crappy in the end?

All of these are hilltop destinations on our daily drive. They tax our engine and bring us close to overheating. It makes sense to ask, "Is the destination worth the effort?"

But removing all hills from your itinerary is not the only way to keep your temperature in check. In fact it is more of a band-aid than a real solution. Far more important is working on the engine until it is running smooth. Ideally it can handle the steep inclines without running too hot.

Plus, there are some amazing destinations on the top of pretty steep hills. So avoiding inclines altogether is not a very realistic solution. It is MUCH better to have the option to go where you please.

And you can do this with a well-maintained and healthy running engine.

In some ways our mind engine is extremely complicated. There are an infinite number of thoughts that can give it trouble. Most of these can be categorized as either fear, guilt or regret.

It is best to deal with them as they arise. Brush them away daily before they gum anything up. But this daily maintenance is a change from the way most of us have been trained.

Most people have a hospital-style attitude about the engine. They only bring it in for maintenance when the "Check Engine" light goes on. Or worse yet, when they break down on the side of the road. Most people have the same attitude about their Happiness. It is only things like prolonged depression that spur people to "look under their hood."

But by that time the fear thoughts have settled in deep into the gears. We develop patterns and bad habits. Each one adding more friction to the engine's workings (and building up more heat & stress.)

It is much more helpful to do minor engine maintenance every day. Check the dial each morning. Brush away any unnecessary debris.

This daily maintenance can be different for each person. Some popular tasks are exercise, meditation, gratitude lists, reading books, or listening to lectures from more experienced mental mechanics.

The key is shifting from the passive, "I'm having a bad day" to an empowered, "What am I thinking that is making me unhappy?" Until we can read the dials, it feels like our mental state is out of our hands.

But when we start to check our mental dashboard, we gain a whole new level of control over our lives.

Simply knowing you are having stressful thoughts doesn't mean you can wave your hand and make them go away, but it is a start.

If I am feeling anxious or unhappy, it can be difficult to recognize. I can easily drive my car all day and not realize it is running hot. But as I work on my maintenance schedule, I am getting better at noticing when things are off. Often simply knowing to check the dials is the hardest part.

Once I know to check in with myself, I can usually see the fear, guilt or regret thoughts. Invariably it is because I am either: 1) Not being present or 2) Feeling separate or 3) being attached to an outcome.

Once I can pull back and see the less-than-happy thoughts that I am having, it is easy to address them.

Of course, pursuing peace of mind with those 3 diagnoses can be journeys unto themselves. Entire spiritual paths are dedicated to each and they can take lifetimes to master. This should not be discouraging – on the contrary! This can be one of the most empowering revelations an individual can have.

Going from passively "accepting" your mental state to having active control over it is a massive shift. We still need to read the maintenance manual and do the work, but until we know how to check the dials, it is impossible to know where to start.

The Game(s) of Life

"What would you do if you knew you would not fail?"
- Popular motivational mantra.
"What would you do if you knew you would not win?"
-Jacob Glass' corrected version of the mantra.

Life is a Game.

But there are two distinct cultural games being played simultaneously. And the rules are totally at odds.

By far the most popular game is "Outwardly Mobile." This is essentially the national sport.

The objective of this game is material success. On the back cover of the box is a picture of a heterosexual family with kids, a house, a summer home, and a boat. The deluxe version includes a white picket fence, an extensive stock portfolio, and a golden retriever.

The rules of the game are simple:

The color of your game piece is chosen for you based on a dice roll that occurs before the game begins. Generally it is some version of "brown."

Based on a few more random rolls of the dice, you select what type of character you'll be in the game. The types have many different names (called, "titles" or "careers") but they basically are broken down into "white collar" or "blue collar."

Each type of character must perform a series of tasks in exchange for tokens. When you collect enough tokens, you can exchange them for "Comfort Goods" or "Status Goods."

Depending on your Title and how the dice rolls turn out, you may chase Comfort Goods for the entire game. (You are supposed to satisfy your Comfort Goods needs before you get Status Goods.)

According to the back of the box, if you never get enough tokens to get Status Goods, you lose.

But if by shrewd game play or lucky dice rolling you attain lots of tokens, you can start accumulating Status Goods. Some of these, like the popular "SUV" Token, can be displayed to taunt your opponents. Other tokens, like "401K" & "Stock Portfolio" are used to create an invisible force field of security.

It is very difficult, if not impossible, to win the game without a force field. Unfortunately it is unclear how big a force field is required. You can spend the entire game in a state of panic because you are uncertain about your force field's strength. Not only that, but there are a number of game obstacles (like "Health problem" and "Car Accident") that can go right through a force field.

Still, the game is fairly straight forward. The players with the most tokens and Status Goods are considered winners.

There is an obscure rule called "Shooting the Moon" that, despite being incredibly difficult, has become an immensely popular way to play. To shoot the moon you must roll an odds-defying number of double 6 rolls and attain the title of "Celebrity." Unfortunately, you can waste a huge portion of the game going for double sixes without ever getting many tokens. But if you do Shoot the Moon, you automatically win.

The basic rules boil down to math. More=better. However, If you play long enough, you'll find that the number of obscure (and seemingly unfair) rules are significant. Many players spend their final rounds of the game frustrated and disgusted. Some even decide to quit and play the other –far less popular- game.

The other game is called, "Inward Peace."

First off, this game is not held in very high regard by the government or culture at large. Most people assume that people only play this game because they suck at the more important "Outwardly Mobile" game.

It is true that most Inward Peace players are defectors from the more popular game. But this could be simply because Inward Peace is not advertised much and so most people don't know about it. You have to ask for it behind the counter or be introduced to it by a friend. It doesn't have a fancy board or expensive gear, and so is easy to overlook.

On first glance, it may not seem like a game at all. In fact, the minute you start playing you are told that have already won.

If you have been playing "Outwardly mobile" for a long time, this may be impossible to grasp. Or more often, downright offensive. No tokens!? It certainly is harder to make sense of than the simple math of "Outward Mobile."

If the game is already won, then how do we spend all our time!? Some people chose to return to the Outwardly Mobile game – in essence playing both games at once. This can make it much less stressful to play Outward Mobile when we know deep down we have already won.

Other people embrace the "Inward Peace" bonus round. This round lasts as long as you like, has no obstacles, and is more like a sand box to play in than a course to race on.

If you have been playing "Outward Mobile" for a long time, this bonus round can seem insane.

But for those who dedicate themselves to "Inward Peace" and practice daily, the exact opposite is true.

In the end we have a culture full of Outwardly Mobile *and* Inwardly Peaceful – both thinking the other has completely missed the point.

The truth is, we can only judge our own paths. We can only play our own game. And the way we roll our dice and move our pieces is entirely up to us.

Groundhog Day & The Power of Now

I love anything that Bill Murray is in. Stripes, Ghostbusters, Meatballs, Scrooged, etc.. He is one of those rare comedic actors who can make me start smiling with just a facial expression.

Last night "Groundhog Day" was playing on Bravo. So, of course, I watched. I'm not sure why it is so much more compelling to watch movies when they are playing live on TV. I'll often watch a film on TV – with commercials – even when I own the DVD somewhere in my collection. I think it has something to do with the collective viewing experience. Even though we are in different physical locations, there is a crowd of people all watching at the same time. It is like a communal theatre experience – without the sticky floor.

In any case, I watched Groundhog Day last night along with 1000's of strangers. The neat thing about that movie is that you can miss the beginning and not get too lost – since the movie consists of the same day happening over and over again.

If you have not seen it, Netflix it, immediately. The premise is that a grumpy weatherman named Phil finds himself living the same day over and over again. Every morning he wakes up at 6am on Groundhog Day. No matter what happens during the day, when he goes to sleep, he wakes up at 6am and it is the beginning of Groundhog Day. Again.

It's an awesome premise that gives a stage for Murray's antics. But it is also a perfect scenario to illustrate some deep spiritual ideas. As I re-watched the film last night, I saw a beautiful new depth to it.

** ALERT: SPOILERS BELOW **

At the start of the movie, Murray's character is unhappy, selfish, and inconsiderate.

Despite the fact that his worldview makes him miserable, he believes he knows best.

Phil is the Everyman of the modern world: Ego absorbed and suffering – but with no willingness to change. In essence being unhappy because he is too stubborn to accept that he may not have it all figured out. He would rather be right about how lame everything is than be happy.

The beginning of the movie paints the picture of this person: Miserable on the inside and miserable to be around. He is stuck in a lame small town and everything seems to be an obstacle – even though he has no clear destination.

Things get interesting when he wakes up the next morning, and it is Groundhog Day, once again. He goes through the day, everyone and everything says and acts exactly as the day before. Much Bill Murray silliness ensues.

Once the shock dies down, Murray's character starts to think of ways he can take advantage of the situation. Since he knows he will wake up tomorrow in the same place/day, he starts to learn about people so that he can manipulate them. He learns where a pretty girl goes to high school so that he can manufacture a disarming ice breaker (and eventually sleep with her.)

This is the Ego steering it's way through the world. He acts selfishly to get what he wants – often at the expense of others. This is the "dog-eat-dog" mentality that we fall into so often. We step on others to get what we want, never realizing that the rewards we gain rarely make us happy.

He symbolizes the stage of awareness of trying to change the world to fit our image of happiness. He imagines that he would be happy if he could get the girl, so he sets on changing the circumstances of the world to get what his Ego mind wants. Of course, since he gets an infinite number of do-overs, he is pretty successful.

The movie shows him altering his seduction script with each failed attempt. At one point she yells at him and rather than respond to her, he makes a mental note to himself, "No fudge and no white chocolate. Got it."

He goes through round after round of this day, each time getting closer to crafting it perfectly. Or at least perfectly crafted according to his Plan.

And yet, he never reaches the happy scenario he strives for.

Just like in real life, the Ego often has no idea what will actually make us happy – even if we think we do. The problem is that the Ego, by it's nature, acts from a selfish place. Even if it gets what it wants, it is operating from a place lacking love and peace. It is like the businessman who does what it takes to get the promotion, get the house and car, does everything according to plan and then realizes, "My God, what have I done?" I have achieved my image of Happiness – and yet I am not happy!

Phil falls deep into the Victim role.

He feels powerless and becomes depressed. He is trapped on the wheel of suffering.

For the Ego mind, and all it's plans, the fact that tomorrow never comes is the worst possible nightmare. Nothing matters and nothing will change.

Finally, he decides to kill himself. Repeatedly.

He crashes his car, electrocutes himself, and jumps off a building. Each time he wakes up at 6am on Groundhog Day.

This is the symbolic killing off of his ego. Stripping away all his desires.

Until finally he says, "I've killed myself so many times, I don't even exist any more."

He says this like it is a bad thing, but it is only from this place of non-existent ego that his transformation takes place.

In essence, he surrenders.

He no longer tries to manipulate things for his own good. Instead he begins to speak honestly from the heart without an agenda.

He introduces several hobbies to his life: Taking piano lessons and learning ice sculpting. These create entertaining plot points, but they symbolize the daily practice and discipline of a spiritual path.

We also see him demonstrate a non-attachment to material goods. He has learned all-too-vividly that "you can't take it with you." We see him be incredibly generous at every opportunity.

Without any hope for a future, his life/day becomes about what is the best way he can contribute in this moment.

In fact, Generosity and Giving become his sole purpose. He makes his daily practice about helping people. Since he knows everything that happens on this day perfectly, he walks around town and is available to help when each obstacle (that he knows is coming) arises. He changes a tire, applies the Heimlich maneuver, and catches a kid who falls from a tree. Service becomes his daily practice.

His demeanor finally becomes calm as he surrenders to this infinite Now. For Phil, the "Now" that Eckard Tolle talks about has become quite literal.

Without the legacy of his past story, he is free to be anyone.

Without the expectations of the future, he is free to do anything.

After much trial and error, he finally embraces a "Love more, fear less. Float more, steer less" mentality.

He surrenders to the Now. He follows Love. He is free of Fear.

From this place, Joy and Love flow effortlessly into his life.

His evolution is complete and the "curse" is finally lifted when he says, "Whatever happens tomorrow, I am happy Now."

Within the confines of a single day, in a small town, we witness a life-long spiritual path play out. From Selfishness, to Dispair, to loss of Ego. We witness the wheel of suffering and see the importance of a daily practice, selflessness, and service. Finally, he Surrenders fully to the Now and finds Joy.

From this place, it makes no difference how many more weeks of winter the groundhog predicts. Every Now moment is perfect.

It makes me wonder how many comedies of my youth can be appreciated from a spiritual level? Maybe we should try some Pauley Shore movies next??? Maybe not.

Turtlenecks & Fake Tans

"It is better to live your own destiny imperfectly than to live an imitation of somebody else's life with perfection."
~The Bhagavad Gita

A long time ago I had the realization that trying to be something that you are not is infinitively more stressful than allowing yourself to be what you are.

In many ways it is the difference between floating and steering.

I can remember years and years of awkward struggles. Trying to be cool. Trying to be liked. Trying to look how I should or react in the right way.

Living like that is no fun. It is like constantly being on stage and trying to impress the audience.

Something interesting happens when you try to be something you are not – and fail. Yes, It feels terrible. It is embarrassing. For a young adult, this can be the most painful judgment imaginable.

But the interesting part is that in that situation, we are not being judged for what we are – we are being judged for failing to be something that we are not.

There were kids at my school who embraced their individuality. They dressed how they wanted, acted how they wanted and decided they wanted no part in the reindeer games of the cool kids.

But I was not strong enough to be one of those kids. I probably even mocked them.

I wanted to be cool. Every clothing purchase was 20% "How do I like it?" And 80% "Will people like it? " Often it was an even more fearful question, "Will this get me teased?"

This went way beyond clothing. I can remember evaluating a girl's attractiveness based on her social standing.

I can remember deciding that I hated a band because that was general attitude about them at my school.

I look back at that time and wonder, who was I? I was living defensively. I was living in fear that my act would be compromised and people would realize that the person who had infiltrated the cool clique was a fraud.

Insanity.

I lived in stress and fear so that I could be someone that I was not. And the reward? Acceptance by other people living charades. Or more accurately: non-ridicule.

When I was in Jr. high, my complexion did its puberty thing like most the other kids. I would obsess about every blemish. I would go into a sort of trance in front of the mirror – picking and popping everything I could find.

My mildly poor complexion was made quite awful due to my picking. My skin tone would take on a splotchy pink every time I would go on a picking rampage. Which is to say my skin was generally a splotchy pink.

I used "skin-tone" Clearasil on the larger red marks I created.

Eventually I reached a tipping point and decided that wearing women's makeup would be less humiliating than walking around in my splotchy skin.

And so I began wearing foundation or powder to even out my skin and hide the effects of my facial picking.

This was an incredibly terrifying time for me. My charade had never been so transparent. I was wearing the evidence right there on my face – and I lived in constant fear of someone noticing that I wore makeup.

I would surely be labeled a "fag." (Which would have been a fate worse than death.)

About this same time I also became obsessed by how skinny my neck was compared to my massive ears. Luckily, I came up with a solution: Wear a turtle neck. Wearing a turtle neck hid my skinnyness and minimized how much my ears stuck out. Problem solved!

Looking back I am shocked at my insanity. I wore a winter turtle neck (alone or with a shirt over it) EVERY DAY. As the days got warmer, I would wear turtle necks with shorts and try not to overheat.

But the turtle necks compounded another one of my worries: What if my face makeup got on the turtle neck?! Oh what a tangled web we weave, when we first start to deceive…

I lived in fear of the discovery, but it never happened.

A year later, I discovered (and became obsessed with) fake tanning cream.

The fake tan would tint my pink blotches and made me feel much better about my skin.

Until one day a friend asked publically, "Dude, why is your skin so orange!?"

I remember the moment vividly. It felt like I was shot in the chest. I was terrified. I was petrified. My heart felt like it jumped into my throat and I could feel my face flush. I eeked out, "I don't know,"and scuttled off before anyone else could investigate his statement.

I may have even gone home. I know that I thought my world had collapsed. The worst possible thing I could imagine had happened.

Someone discovered that I was not the person I had been pretending to be.

I eased up on the tan crème, softened the orange with some pressed powder makeup, and prepared for social Armageddon. But as is often the case with adolescence, I misjudged how much people cared or paid attention to me. My friend didn't mention it again and neither did anyone else.

Still, I lived in fear of the other shoe dropping. I avoided pool parties and took extra care to ensure my turtle necks would not be stained around the collar.

About this time I saw my friend Scott demonstrate a type of courage I had never seen before. During some mean-natured ribbing, he resisted the instinct to defend himself or fight back.

Instead he said, "Wow, it really hurts my feelings when you say things like that."

BAM!

This was a revolution.

It stunned the aggressor and stopped the teasing. Suddenly the crowd's perception was that the aggressor was being a jerk.

Scott had decided not to play the game. He refused to maintain the charade. Instead he stood strongly in his truth and confessed his weakness.

But in claiming it as his own, he was not made weaker at all. On the contrary, he gained power. Suddenly the attacks were deflected.

This demonstration changed everything for me and set into motion a quest towards introspective honesty that continues today.

Soon after, someone did notice my odd skin tone. But I didn't panic. Instead I replied what I had practiced in my mind. "Yes, I use fake tanning lotion."

They was a minor joke at my expense, but it had no power to it. Standing in truth, there was no weapon to use against me. By claiming the rock as my own, I left only tiny pebbles to throw at me.

If I'm trying to perpetuate a fraud, then it is humiliating to get caught.

But if I simply am what I am, then what power does discovery hold? Sure they can still tease me for this truth, but it holds a fraction of the impact.

There is a line in "The Course in Miracles" that reads, "In my defenselessness, my safety lies."

Sometimes I imagine the lion Aslan surrendering to the evil forces of Narnia. Or Jesus carrying his cross. They refused to fight back and in doing so became infinitely more powerful.

Years later, when I discovered the web and global self-publishing, I returned to this idea. The Internet became a digital confessional for me.

The more I would reveal about supposed "weakness," the more support I felt from readers. The more vulnerable I allowed myself to be, the more powerful I became.

People sometimes commended my bravery, but they misunderstood the grand equation. I was not showing my weakness to the enemy – I was removing the weapon from their arsenal. Once I have told you that I am insecure about my complexion, it is no longer a rock you can throw at me. The activists who chose the name "Queer Nation" understood this.

But the real epiphany has much more to do with the internal awareness than any outside attacks. If you are trying to play a role, then you are set up to fail.

If I am trying to be cool, and then someone decides that I am not, it hurts. This pain is deeper than the ridicule, itself. It hurts because I have tried to steer a situation and create a perception – but I have failed.

Contrast this with standing in your truth and being ridiculed for that. You may prefer to be liked, but really, what does that have to do with you? If you are being who you are, then how people respond is none of your business. If you act from truth you CANNOT fail. Truth is truth. Does a mountain fail because it doesn't have enough trees? Only a crazy person would think that. And it is the same type of childish perspective that would judge a person for their truth.

When we sit in our truth with confidence, judgment cannot touch us. Because the judgment – by definition – comes from a place much lower than truth. It comes from weakness. And by choosing not to defend against it, it remains outside of our world entirely.

Buddha taught that if someone hands you a gift and you do not accept, then the gift remains in their possession. The same is true with insults and judgment. It does not have to be a part of your world at all.

In my defenselessness, my safety lies.

In contrast to what we might think, a person who does not defend can be infinitely powerful. Look at leaders like MLK Jr. or Gandhi. They transcended their physical power because they surrendered to ultimate vulnerability. You can beat my body. You can imprison me. But you cannot deny me my truth. From this defenseless truth, the frailest of beings can change the world.

More importantly, we can free our minds.

God In A Dewdrop

I don't resonate with the idea of an external God that is separate from me.

For me, there is only The One. There is only God. There is only The Universe.

It is one infinite, perfect equation. Stardust to embryo to earthquake to atom.

Somewhere in the middle of this massive equation is our planet.

And somewhere in the lifetime of this planet is our species.

And somewhere in the middle (end?) of this species' run is my current consciousness.

I am like a water particle that helps form a rainbow.

Could I ever hope to understand the rainstorm that preceded me? Or the sunlight that refracts me? Yet, could I define myself without the rain or sun? What about the snowfall last season that melted into the lake that evaporated and became the rain?

My grandfather used to call God, among other things, "the Unbegun Beginning."

I wish I understood that phrase more when he was alive. But I think I get it now. This infinite equation is the Unbegun Beginning. The Universe is a Mobius strip. Our human perception of time makes us see our lives through tunnel vision which leads to thinking that somehow we are separate and isolated from the rest of the equation.

It is ironic that the human traits we are so proud of: Our intellect, personality and consciousness – are responsible for this perception of separation.

Of course, we are not really separate – but our Ego convinces us that we are alone in the world. And therefore we need to struggle and plan in order to forge our path. We are driven to stand out, fix things, and make a difference.

But as the Buddhist story explains – it is like a wave thinking it is separate from the sea.

It would be humorous if it were not so tragic.

This separation is what leads to so much of the horror in our world. Not just in the way we allow ourselves to treat other parts of the equation (like the environment, other species, or fellow humans) but in the way we torture ourselves with thoughts.

How painful to believe that it is "Me against the world." What a setup for stress and suffering. And yet, this is a very common belief system. How much more peaceful to understand, "Me is a part of the world."

Of course, part of this awareness is understanding that "I" will die. And that, too, is a perfect part of the equation. The Mobius strip includes birth, death, decay, rebirth. We should feel honored to be a part of these cycles, not frustrated by our impermanence.

If you see the universe as a Mobius strip, then all moments exist forever. No matter how long we are alive, no matter when, we are a part of the equation. We are a part of the One.

It is our Ego that freaks out over the thought of death. Which makes some sense, because it is only our ego that dies. The Ego is that part of us that feels separate. The part of us that is a part of the infinite cosmic One exists now and forever. Our true self cannot die because it was never born.

The thing that was born into this body is the Ego – the awareness of separation or "self." I would argue that this awareness is a sickness that afflicts the human species. It may even prove to be an evolutionary handicap.

This belief of separateness allows for natural destruction that could eventually make our planet uninhabitable to humans (and many other species.)

Every animal species that survives settles into a harmony within the Equation. (Or at least the tiny fraction of the equation that works itself out on Earth in the Milky Way corner of the cosmic blackboard.)

Too voracious an appetite, the species decimates it's food supply and in turn dies out. This is not good or bad. This is just how the equation works. It is perfect and beautiful.

From this awareness, the entire natural world becomes a university & monastery. I find nature documentaries to be incredible spiritual tools in helping to deeply feel this Unbegun Beginning. As Carl Sagan or Richard Attenburrough or whatever cool-voiced narrator explains the bizarre checks and balances of the physical world, I find myself awash in Awe.

The big monkey brain feels some need to compartmentalize and explain this situation. But an explanation will not bring peace.

More important is appreciation and awe. If we can sink into a state of awe at the universe, then it becomes easy to slip into a state of gratitude.

We do not need to understand the fusion on the sun's surface to appreciate the warmth on our skin.

"Nothing thinks greater than the creator's thoughts" is another thing my grandpa would say often.

And this is more of how I view my relationship with God. My consciousness is not in the driver's seat of the universe. It is not my role to "understand" it all. I just need to allow myself to appreciate the gift of existence: I am a part of the cosmic equation. I am a part of the One.

I am a dewdrop reflecting God to the universe.

Beautiful.

Forgive Me, Jesus

I had an awesome lunch yesterday with a exceptionally wise Christian friend. As we talked I found myself finding more connection with Jesus' words as well as clarity of basic spiritual ideas I have been exploring.

Preface: I am not a Christian. I see Jesus as a great Spiritual leader who tried to express a profound divine awareness with those around him. He tried to put the awareness into words (Which have then been translated and passed on through the Multi-generational Church PR machine.) But I think the specific words are far less important than the direction of the ideas.

And to me, I see this same direction of thought from many evolved teachers in history and living today.

So, while I am frustrated by some people's strict allegiance to the words of the bible, I am also struck by how often it can be interpreted in ways that mesh perfectly with my "new age" philosophies.

For example, I see Jesus as the role model for our ideal selves. I don't see him as the son of God but as a symbol of the divine in all of us. In this sense, we "follow Jesus" as we walk our paths and strip away our worldly socialization. The false idols we need to avoid are the "gods " of status, fame, wealth, etc..

Chasing these things is a sure fire path to suffering. And if we place these things above Love, our world feels like it is filled with obstacles and injustice. This focus on "what is wrong" is what I would call, "Hell."

But when we see the miracles that surround us, then Heaven is in every moment.

Therefore the "path" to heaven is within. Or "Through me, " meaning "becoming more Christ-like."

I was thinking about the almost comical Christian belief that you can ask for forgiveness on your deathbed and no matter what you did, still go to Heaven.

But during lunch I had an epiphany: This idea of instant access to Heaven through forgiveness is profound.

The reality is that you are not asking forgiveness of anything outside of yourself. You are accepting the flawed perfection that is "you."

You are recognizing that this Ego Persona is not really, "You." All these things you may have shame or guilt over, were done as part of your separate ego identity. But when you let go of that identity – when you "forgive" that part of yourself – then you can step into your divine one-ness.

And THAT puts you in the state of Heaven in an instant.

In that moment that we recognize that ANY decision we make with our ego minds is severely limited, we are set free.

"Forgiveness" of the ego self is a recognition of non-separation.

If we let go of our ego identity, then we can sense the one-ness of the universe: the connection with all things.

It is also a release of attachment – a letting go of that perception that we know what is best.

My ego brain is not to be trusted. As I ask forgiveness for the actions of my Ego self, I am surrendering to a higher power, flow, energy, love, God.

I see this forgiveness as the same sort of awakening. An awakening where the divine seed in us "forgives" the ego mind for it's narrow choices and actions.

"Accepting Jesus in our heart" is actually a surrendering to the divine connection that has always existed within us.

And suddenly the idea of being absolved of all sins in an instant makes a ton of sense.

"Go with the Flow" is an oft misunderstood phrase.

It doesn't mean to do what others' around are doing. Or to avoid conflict.

It is not passiveness.

On the contrary, the Flow is universal strength.

Water is a perfect example of this.

A body of water will yield to the touch and a droplet will take the path of least resistance.

But do not confuse this willingness to compromise for weakness. If you have ever stood on the edge of the Grand Canyon, you have witnessed the immense power of water.

I use the phrase "Float more, steer less." to remind myself of this principle.

Some people confuse this with apathy or laziness.

Not so.

Floating doesn't meat motionless. Floating means that your direction comes from a place much bigger than you.

Rather than picking a destination and powering your way through every obstacle to get there, you go deep and feel the direction that you are being pulled. Then swim in that direction.

You still use effort. You still work hard. You just do so in the direction of universal flow. And so go much farther with much less effort.

To do this, you need to let go of the belief that you know what the best outcome is.

This is massive.

Way too often we claw our way towards an objective. We bite, scratch, and step on heads to get the promotion, parking place, or position we believe we need to be content.

There is a HUGE difference between wanting to *be* content and wanting to get *what you believe* will make you content.

I would argue this is one of the core challenges our culture faces.

This disconnect is the very basis of marketing and the advertising-based culture we are submerged in every day.

Floating can also take FAR more courage than swimming towards traditional goals. Because who is to say that the cosmic current takes you in the direction of a wife, kids and picket fence?

You can always force your way, paddling and splashing against the flow. This is the situation with so many gay people pressured to live in the closet.

After Burning Man, I was living in a webcam house and intentionally attacking all the false currents I could find. I aggressively confronted the societal pressures to dress a certain way or pursue a certain path or keep certain parts of your life private.

In today's world of Twitter and status updates, it does not seem so revolutionary. But in 2000, living transparently online was a novelty left to puppies.

I moved in with five members of my Burning Man camp to TheRealHouse.com and we made living transparently into an art project.

At the same time, "WeLiveInPublic" was happening in New York with a much bigger budget and with much more traditional "success."

One thing we learned quickly was how powerfully oppressed most of us are about our sexuality.

Merely speaking openly about sex can be seen as subversive. So to allow one's sex life to be viewed, discussed, and celebrated – well, that was too much for most.

I was told, "Sex is sacred and therefore should be private."

But this doesn't make any sense to me.

Religion is sacred. Yet we make worship into a public event every Sunday. (You could easily argue that what we see in many of these churches is far from sacred – but that is a separate point.)

My open sexuality at the time brought me lots of detractors. I had won a Webby award the year before and had my share of "fans." But I "went too far," many said.

I kept coming back to "float more."

Maybe it was *because* of all the obstacles, but I felt compelled to continue in this risqué direction. Our puritanical oppression was not a wall to flow around, but a jagged rock that needed to be softened.

The status quo wanted us to swim (fully clothed) in the direction of traditional morality and levels of public sharing.

But the cosmic flow pulled in the other direction. My house-mates and I let the universe steer and started paddling in the direction of the flow.

It is during those times of flow when everything seems to come together. You are in the right place at the right time. You meet the right people. Synchronicity follows you everywhere.

Nature As Sacred Text

I have been devouring science documentaries.

To me, studies of the natural world are better tools for studying "God" than sacred texts.

A Sacred text is a man's attempt to put the inexpressible into words. Often those words are then translated. Sometimes the original words are even passed down several times before they make it into print.

Language is an amazing tool. But it is merely a tool. Remember in high school when your writing professor would repeat the mantra, "show don't tell"?

Don't tell me the flower was pretty, show me it's beauty. Describe the colors and patterns and the play of the light.

But even the greatest poet could not accurately convey the baffling beauty of a orchid. Joyce Kilmer wrote long ago, *"I think that I shall never see a poem lovely as a tree..."*

And this is the trouble with sacred words. They are all, essentially, poems about trees.

I don't mean to argue their truth or value – only to point out the obvious limitations of words.

After reading a particularly vivid account of an experience – say surviving the Katrina floods – you might feel as though you had been there. But it would be incredibly naive to believe that you had the same experience as someone who was neck deep in water and fear.

Could you ever read enough about giving birth to reach an understanding of what that experience is like? Or having sex?

To me, studying science on a very surface level is not about understanding. I have no goal of learning the details of fusion or the intricacies of photosynthesis. Instead, the basic knowledge serves to pulverize into mush any lingering need my brain has of making sense of it all.

Understanding how it all works = impossible and stressful.

Surrendering to the infinitely complex order = calming and peaceful.

This is particularly helpful if you combine micro and macro learning. From microscope to telescope. From distant galaxy to inside my body.

No matter how far my attention goes in any direction it never stops uncovering incomprehensible levels of order, chaos, drama, and interconnectedness.

The human drama with its adultery, career paths, and invention is no more complicated or important than the drama of a marshland biosphere or a distant pulsar.

The universe is fractal-y amazing.

The more I watch COSMOS or the Discovery Channel, the more giddy I become with awe.

It seems to me that this awe and appreciation is immensely more important than understanding.

I can enjoy a roller coaster without understanding the physics. I just have faith that the track is constructed in such a way that it supports the speed, gravity, and torque of the ride.

I could read a book about how the ride should be ridden. I could follow the exact steps a legendary rider of the past took: Commandment 4: Thou shall not eat multiple corn dogs before riding. Commandment 5: Thou shall be taller than this sign. Commandment 6: On the Sabbath, lines are longer so try to go mid-week. Etc.

The rules & descriptions can certainly be helpful. But they must be understood in their place. Too many people are reading the rules AS they are riding – so focused on the abstract that they are not enjoying the actual experience.

It may sound trite to suggest to someone that they stop to smell the flowers. But on the contrary, this is profound spiritual guidance.

For me, the natural world holds direct glimpses into the divine. Like a more literal biblical God, it is not something I can look directly at – it is simply too much for me to comprehend. But in every veined leaf I see the reflection of this divine order.

The ego wills of humans – my own included – disintegrate into comical naiveté.

In a universe so overwhelmingly miraculous, I have been given the ability to perceive it. My purpose is no more (or less) grandiose than any other piece of the cosmic puzzle whether massive star or tiny atom.

But what IS significant – more so than anything else that defines my existence – is that I am able to perceive and ponder this miracle as it unfolds.

It is a unique human gift. And our appreciation of this gift defines our life and our relationships with all other life.

Of course, it is pretty ridiculous to try to explain all of this with words.

"I think that I shall never see…"

Upside Down Maslow

Dmitry and I were in the airport checking in. As we waited in line, we discussed how being a seeker is a luxury. And how our parent's generations did not seek "fulfillment" or "bliss."

I explained Maslow's "Hierarchy of Needs" from what I remembered of Intro to Psych.

First you need food and shelter, then safety, then love, until finally- at the top – is Self Actualization.

According to Maslow, you have to fill your lower needs before you can begin to fill the higher ones. You cannot seek love while running from a bear. And you must put food on the table before you can think about self actualization.

"But that is wrong!" Dmitry said.

And the more we discussed it, the clearer it got.

You should not postpone your joy while you seek security.

This has become one of the key frauds pulled on our culture. We are taught that working hard as we work our way up Maslow's hierarchy will eventually give us enough of a financial cushion that we can find peace and relaxation in our retirement.

But it doesn't work that way.

We live in a culture overflowing with resources and luxury. We have personal computers, vibrating car seats, and hot running water. So why are so many of us stuck in the middle of the pyramid?

First of all, something crazy happened to the security needs tier.

There was a time when having a roof over your head and food were legitimate needs. But as more and more people got those needs met, we didn't culturally ascend to the next level. Instead we kept inventing more and more needs.

We were struck by an epidemic societal plague: Marketing.

Rather than evolve up the ladder once our needs were met, we taught ourselves an infinite number of new needs.

It only takes an hour's worth of Television and its commercials to illustrate this:

"Does your ladder do THIS!?"

"Embarrassed by your pale elbows?"

"Our list of 10 celebs who are NOT ready for swimsuit season...coming up next! But now a word from our sponsor..."

We are bombarded with messages that we are not enough. We lack. We need fixing.

Luckily for us, we are also given an endless number of solutions...available in 3 installments of 19.95 (plus S&H).

Is my TV big enough? flat enough? Are the blacks black enough?

Are my teeth white enough? Is my butt firm enough?

What is even more scary is that marketing, undeniably works. And not just with products. We are susceptible to it in politics and sadly, with religion, too.

On some Sunday mornings, you can not tell the difference between a Ginsu knife commercial and a call to prayer. They are both filled with urgency, optimism, and a guarantee that sending in your money will make your life (and afterlife) unfathomable better.

So what happens when the second-to-top tier continues to expand? We become like Sisyphus, pushing a stone that rolls back down the mountain each night. Every time we acquire, there is some new need popping up ahead of us.

And even when our house is full of the latest gadgets in the hippest colors, we still do not climb upward. The big trick is that there is no "enough." Since true security is a myth, you can never have enough saved to guarantee your safety.

If you can't let go of the need for security, you are stuck in the hierarchy.

Martha Beck said the number one fear of her clients is fear of being homeless. Sacrificing the majority of your life to work you don't like and the rest of your life to a state of fear is a pretty high price to pay.

But that is what we do if we can't rattle up Maslow's need structure.

This is what Jesus taught.

A rich man would have an easier time getting into heaven than a camel through the eye of a needle.

Buddha taught this, too. And many more prophets and gurus who teach that danger of worldly attachment.

But what if we did mess with the structure.

What if we put self actualization FIRST.

If you were at one with the universe, even running from a bear could be a pleasant experience.

So would acquiring shelter, and providing food.

Every task in your life could be done from an entirely different place.

The same actions, except motivated without the same fear.

Well, not the exact same actions, because from the self-actualized state, you would not want to deceive or harm others. You would not want to sacrifice the environment for your personal gain. You would feel a sense of connection and so would act in the service of the world, even while satisfying your own interests.

Now, this isn't to say that a self actualized worker will be more "successful" in the societally-defined sense. Many rich people acquire great wealth through cut-throat practices and selfishness.

And turning away from the traditional goals of financial security can be seemingly catastrophic. You *could* lose all your stuff.

But if you are living in fear because you don't have enough or will lose what you have, then your stuff is infinitely too expensive.

That being said, it gets complicated when you have kids. But not really.

People argue that they work so hard to provide security for their children. And while this is an admirable goal, it doesn't make sense. If a child has a fancy roof over their head but learns the deep rooted lesson that life is about struggle, lack, and always being in need...well then that child has been raised in poverty.

The same kid, raised in a van down by the river could grow up feeling all his needs were always met. And thus grow into a self actualized being, regardless of the state of their financial security.

Does this state of thinking put you at risk for being taken advantage of? Absolutely! They key is to change your perspective on that, too. Jesus said, "And if any man will sue thee at the law, and take away thy coat, let him have thy cloak also."

But when you start slipping into a one-ness mentality, then you never lose that shirt. It just moves to another part of you. In fact, the act if giving that shirt to the other person can be one of the most profound spiritual acts you can do.

Nature & Sin

While I love the idea of "getting back to nature," I recognize that nature is a vicious place.

Most of the creatures on the earth spend their time trying to 1) avoid being killed, 2) finding enough food so they don't die, and 3) having enough sex so that their species can continue.

This is a far cry from the calm breathing, and babbling brooks that we often imagine when the word "nature" is uttered.

The natural order of things is aggression. It is perfect in its balance…but it is not peaceful.

Evolution is NOT about "Survival of the most compassionate."

Even human children, while beautiful and perfect, also have the seed of aggression.

This capacity to resort to violence is our "original sin."

Of course, there is nothing sinful about it.

In fact, there is perhaps nothing more natural.

You don't consider a hawk sinful for killing a mouse, do you?

So it is silly to think of this violent nature as anything but natural.

It would be a pretty evolved hawk that decided that causing harm to another creature was wrong.

It would also be a pretty dead hawk before long.

But the homo sapiens' gift (as well as burden) is that he can train his mind to think outside the natural cycles and patterns.

So, while it may be "natural' to destroy an enemy, one could choose a more righteous path of turning the other cheek.

And although it is perfectly within the natural order of things to eat meat, one could choose to avoid killing animals in an effort to minimize overall suffering.

These are hard choices. But this, I believe, is the true meaning of free will.

Not that we are free to make a choice…

But that our choices can take into consideration concepts far beyond mere survival.

This is what it means to be "made in the image of God."   It means we have a teeny tiny piece of the divine consciousness.

Humans receive the priceless gift of evolved emotional consciousness.

Of course, we are cosmic infants with only a trace of this gift. So we struggle endlessly with our emotions and easily default to the most base (least human) of these, such as fear and anger and judgment.

But the miracle is that we have the capacity for the other end of the consciousness spectrum. The capacity for joy. The capacity for LOVE.

Not just romantic love or sexual love, but divine love.

It is the ability to make choices based in LOVE that is the heart of free will.

It is through these choices that we overcome "original sin."

It is through this higher path that we reach peace/nirvana/heaven.

When Christ said, "I am the way," he was saying, the only way to evolve past the savage cycles of survival is by following in his path.

And the path he demonstrated was one of making choices based on a higher good.

Away from animal dominance and towards pure love.

The Heaven he speaks of is not a place…but an awareness. And Jesus was absolutely right in that we can never attain the awareness while we are tied to earthly things.

Buddha used the word 'attachment' and warned of the suffering that is inherent in the cycles.

Both men, and countless evolved others, said the same thing.

And each teacher tries to find a system that facilitates this unlearning process.

Unlearning the values and patterns of "survival" living – and clearing out the blockages between our animal "mind" and the cosmic consciousness/love/force/source/god.

Our spiritual path is our journey from animal thoughts to god thoughts.

And it takes constant practice.

Love Manifesto

"All you need is Love."

It couldn't be more simple. Yet, it is complicated as hell.

Actually, one could argue that "hell" actually *is* the layers of confusion, ego, and fear that impede the natural flow of Love that is in us.

But our Love essence becomes buried beneath layers and layers as we grow up.

We are socialized from our first breaths.

We are marketed to, not long after.

By the time we are adults, we have no idea who we are.

We know the other type of cola is for old geezers.

We know that the other political party is a bunch of morons.

We know that the people we are fighting are godless terrorists.

We chase carrots without even knowing if we like the taste.

And we know that, in this dog-eat-dog world, too often it comes down to us vs. them.

But none of this has anything to do with who we are. These are stories that we attach to ourselves.

We are simply adopting roles – parent, libertarian, Muslim, poor – and then act accordingly.

But when we strip away our stories…

When we let go of our labels and expectations…

When we peel away the socialization…

We find we are all very much alike.

We all want to love more and fear less.

We are all expressions of Love.

When we can reach this awareness of similarity and oneness, we can begin to feel love towards all.

Your smile makes me smile.

Your joy is my joy.

*And even if you act from one of your stories, I know that deep down, you are perfect and pure. That recognition allows me to have compassion for the false ego self (that happens to be acting like a jerk.)

Death is a Comma

Grandpa was a great role model for dying.

That might sound morbid, but my goodness… if there is ONE thing we can depend on, it's that we will die. The fear and taboo we have about it is not healthy.

Grandpa pointed out to me, that if you asked a fetus if it wanted to come out of the womb, it would say, "Heck, NO!"

So it makes sense that we are also frightened of our *next* transition.

Which is why it was SO WONDERFUL to share Grandpa's final chapter.

It soothed so many of my fears about aging.

He was in great shape for his age. His body held up unbelievably well for 90+ years. Still, he had such a unattached relationship with his "shell."

He would share intimate details with no shame.

They put a tube in my penis…," he started to explain, before seeing me wince. "Hey, this is going be your body someday. You need to know this stuff!"

And he was right. What a gift he was giving me. A glimpse at my genetic future.

He viewed aging with fascination and openness.

He asked a nurse if he could have one of the toilet seat risers installed on his seat.

She was very kind, "Of course, Mr. Shikles! Are your legs giving you trouble getting up and down?"

"Oh no," he said. "My testicles are dipping."

Up until his final year, he was spry and walked quickly. He went on frequent beach walks, daily Jacuzzi, yoga, tai chi.

Except for his daily nap, he was tough to slow down.

During his final year, he was in the hospital a lot with pneumonia.

It wore him out, but never dimmed his light.

And he always bounced back.

The doctors even gave him a surgery they normally would not give a man his age (with multiple bypass surgeries).

But even when he was in the hospital, totally weak and not looking like he was doing too hot, he would be focusing on what was working.

Skipping topics of difficulties and pointing out anything amazing or kind or wonderful. "Look at that tree. What wonderful doctors they have here. The technology is mind-blowing!"

He truly practiced gratitude.

And when the end did come, it came quick. They called hospice in the late evening. The next morning, hospice called and said, you should probably come over.

Mom and I were there.

He was unconscious and breathing heavily.

We held his hand and spoke softly to him.

"It's Okay. We love you. The family is safe. Let go."

I felt so grateful that I had been able to do SO much the last few years. So many conversations. So much video. There was nothing left unsaid.

Well, maybe one thing.

Grandpa had a very special book he loaned me once.

"All Religions Are True" by Gandhi. He got it overseas on travels. It is not in print.

It was the only physical thing of his I wanted. But he had loaned it to someone else recently and I didn't know who.

I looked on his book shelf to see if maybe it was returned.

Nope.

Well, all things considered, I still felt incredibly blessed.

A few minutes later, my mom found a large envelope with my name written in Grandpa's handwriting.

Inside the envelope was the book.

And Grandpa's last breath was not 20 minutes later.

Grandpa's final chapter was the most beautiful thing I have ever witnessed.

Faith

I am beginning to learn what "Faith" means to me.

Faith is about surrender.

From my limited awareness, it seems like many different spiritual paths all teach that surrendering is required for evolution, enlightenment, salvation, etc.

What we surrender to is what defines our Faith.

For me, when I am in my right mind- I surrender to what I would describe as "the Divine flow of the Universe."

- The cosmic equation that maintains constant mass and energy.

- The universal pattern that balances resources through micro and macro cycles.

- The mind-blowing branches of evolutionary life.

Some would call this Tao. Or "The Force." Or Love. Some might have modifications to this and dress it in a human form. Some could wrap this all up under the umbrella of "Science."

***

Whatever it is called, and whatever personality it inhabits, developing a healthy awe of the Universe is critical.

And having Faith is being able to surrender to this awe and recognize that the Divine Flow is beyond our understanding.

Faith is letting go of the belief that a lifetime of consciousness could ever gain the knowledge and experience required to know the best course through the world.

How can we ever logically deduce what our purpose is based on our limited human experience? (Or ALL human experience, for that matter.)

Should we acquire wealth? Create Art? Help Children? Promote Islam? Exterminate Jews?

From the perspective of the Ego, we are always right and "They" are always idiots/heathens/infidels/terrorists.

Every atrocity is committed by someone who believes they are doing the righteous thing.

We say that we want to leave the world better, but how are we to ever know?

With the exception of "adding love to world," what possible change to the world could you KNOW was positive?

We are far too affected by our socialization and culture to trust what our Ego minds define as important. We have no idea if we are being a help or horror. A human lifetime simply has no vantage point.

To charge through the world without understanding the Universe reminds me of the old joke, "I have no idea where we are headed, but we are making great time."

But what if we let go of our Ego plan?

If we look at the rest of the awe-inspiring Universe, it would seem that some sort of harmony and balance would be the Universal model of "Success."

Yet we tend to think that to "win" at the game of life we must rise above and differentiate ourselves. We must make an impact. We must leave the world different.

What kind of desire is this?

It comes from a place of weakness.

It is the same insecurity that drives a powerless youth to spray his name in graffiti on a concrete wall. "I was here."

The same unhealthy impulse drives Trump to blazon his name across massive structures – and drives millions more to aspire to do the same. We want to leave our mark and "tag" the planet.

We want to be noticed and remembered. And in doing so, find ourselves at odds with harmony.

"The reasonable man adapts himself to the world; the unreasonable one persists in trying to adapt the world to himself. Therefore all progress depends on the unreasonable man."

-George Bernard Shaw

We want to be special. We want to stand out. We want to be exceptional.

But we have no reference point to judge what "exceptional" is.

You could argue that cancer cells are exceptional. They make their mark. They make a difference. They stand out from the existing natural systems.

"Every mammal on this planet instinctively develops a natural equilibrium with the surrounding environment but you humans do not. You move to an area and you multiply and multiply until every natural resource is consumed and the only way you can survive is to spread to another area. There is another organism on this planet that follows the same pattern. Do you know what it is? A virus."

-Agent Smith, "The Matrix"

We think that making our mark will make us happy. Research shows that acquiring or accomplishing things does NOT, in fact, increase our happiness. This success we've been sold is snake oil!

(And I won't even get into the fact that – even if you decide to play the traditional Success Game – the deck is totally stacked against you. The game is rigged by the Halliburtons and Enrons of the world.)

So what then?

We've spent our whole life trying to have perfect bodies, the latest gadgets and the coolest car. Even if we say we don't care about those things, we are probably trying to stockpile enough resources so as to reach a mythical state of "security." What do we work towards if not those goals?

This is where it gets tough.

This is where the "real" rules of the game start to emerge – and they are far more difficult to understand than the ones we were raised with.

The challenge is that we have been trained to see life as a competitive playing field, and in reality it is much more like a dance floor.

When we play a game, we are trying to win.

What are we trying to achieve when we hit the dance floor? (Let's assume this is not a singles bar and "getting laid" is not on the agenda.)

There is no "goal" to dancing except to enjoy the experience.

To view life like this seems so simple, but a shift in thinking can be massive and completely unsettling.

This shift is contrary to everything we've been taught and is very hard to surrender to.

Wealth acquisition is an easy math problem. More money = doing better.

It is as easy to understand as the numbers on the scoreboard.

But life is more like a Yoga practice than a baseball game. And there is no scorecard for Yoga. There isn't even colored belts or fancy titles.

You simply practice.

Some days are better than others, but there is no finish line, no victory, and no losing. A yogi simply goes through the flow of postures without an end goal beyond the immediate experience. "Success" in Yoga is the practice itself and the gradual deepening of physical and spiritual experience.

Just as the "Success" of the Universe is its "practice" of cycles and gradual evolution.

Faith, to me, is surrendering to this definition of Success.

I wish it was as easy as making a declaration. How wonderful to scream from a mountaintop , "I surrender to Harmony over Achievement!" and be done with it. Unfortunately, the awareness requires my daily practice. Many times a day, in fact, I need to remind myself of where my Faith is.

Do put my trust in my Ego?

Or do I put my trust in the Universe?

For now, at least, my Faith is tested moment by moment by moment.

10 Gifting Commandments:

Gifting (not bartering) *is one of the founding principals of the Burning Man community. After years of attending, I find that "Gifting" has had a deeply profound affect on me. Here are 10 reasons why:*

1) Gifting is a physical demonstration of Love.

"I want you to have this because it makes me happy to see you happy."

2) Gifting dissolves separation.

When you Gift, you are breaking down the wall between me and you/ us and them. If you EXCHANGE, then you are re-enforcing the separation. But to GIFT is to say, You and I are one.

When I understand the interconnectedness of all things, then Gifting helps to show that I cannot ever lose anything. If I gift you something, I am only transferring it from one part of the One to another. There is no loss and no gain. We are just shifting possession to an aspect of the whole that will appreciate it more. Think "Osmosis of Material Goods."

3) A Gift can be ANYTHING.

It can be a song, an idea, a massage, a sculpture, a compliment, a sticker, a shoulder to lean on, a wet-nap, a walk home, or a hug.

4) Gifting eliminates hoarding and creates abundance.

When we allow "stuff" to flow more fluidly between one another, ALL stuff becomes an available resource to ALL people. Gifting breaks down attachment.

5) Gifting helps dissolve the Ego.

When we become less connected with owning and having stuff (even our skills and talents) then we identify less with our physical selves. We take less credit for things and less blame. Who we are becomes more about our divine seed than our story or physical form.

6) Gifting breaks the commerce paradigm.

Traditional commerce = an even exchange. You get one, I lose one. You pay one, I earn one. Sum total = Zero (0). But in a gift, You receive the gift (+1) AND I feel good for giving the gift (+1). Sum total = Two (2).

7) Gifting releases the flow of energy between people.

We are hardly even aware of the energetic walls that we maintain to hold on to our stuff and keep out yours. The more we gift, the less those barriers hold.

8) Gifting opens up the world.

Making a habit of gifting allows you to see every interaction as an opportunity for increased Joy – even if there is no benefit to you specifically. If I have something (a bite of food, a word of support, a warm hat) that can make your life better, then I can make MY life better by helping YOU. That means there are billions of opportunities in every moment to make the planet more joyful. On the other hand, if the only way to increase joy is by helping out my specific individual self, then the opportunities are few.

9) Gifting is never required.

A feeling of obligation cancels out the Gift. (This type of "Barter" exchange is often confused as gifting.) But if you expect anything in return – even the elimination of guilt – then the magic of Gifting has been compromised.

10) EVERY interaction can be seen as an act of Gifting.

Being A Good Person

How do we learn how to be "good people?"

How do we know what that means?

And how do we know if we are on the right track?

The obvious answer is "parents."

And to a degree, this is true.

But where does the parent learn this?

If your parents didn't teach you, are your kids screwed?

Unfortunately, that seems to be the current system.

Lost people have kids. And raise them as best they can.

But those kids grow into lost people, themselves.

Obviously, that is an over-generalization. It only takes a single caring mentor or a lone meaningful book to change a person's path forever.

But a parent who is caught up in the hamster wheel of modern day material goals is ill-suited to teach an evolved perspective to their kids.

I have much sympathy for a modern parent.

The quest to be a good person is a lifelong one. So how do you begin your role as an instructor while still enrolled in the classes?

My mom was heavily active in church groups while growing up.

My understanding is that these groups were far less about any religious beliefs, and more about values and community.

Helping out those in need was just part of the expected behavior for members of the group. I'm sure this is rooted in Christ's teachings, but the result is independent of specific beliefs.

The result is a value placed on being a good person.

You can knock Christianity all day (and be justified with every blow.) But there are some pretty wonderful ideas to take away from following the teachings of Jesus.

Love thy enemies.

Turn the other cheek.

The meek shall inherit the earth.

If you can let go of your hatred of the things done by Christian institutions, that is some pretty incredible stuff.

My grandpa once told me that if you read nothing else, you can base your life around the teachings of the Sermon on the Mount.

But that still leaves a big vacant hole for those who have discarded traditional religions.

Many westerners find meaning in Eastern religions. Part of the attraction is simply that it is a belief system unmarred by personal experience. We don't know any children molested by Buddhist monks or have any experience with power-hungry Hindu priests.

I'm told that every belief system has corruption once it grows to a significant size.

But if the newness works for you, that's great! If it brings you to a place of love and compassion, then God Bless It!

Unfortunately, I think the majority of people are left without a system to trust.

And so they default to a basic, tribal attitude of 'take care of you and yours…. And screw them before they screw you.'

It may not be so overt. It probably hides inside of white lies and beliefs like, "Someone else would sell them the ___ if I didn't." But there is clearly a disconnect with the Human family.

I have to believe there can be something else.

I have to believe there can be a "Human Family" belief system that teaches people that doing good is its own reward.

It is a shame that most voices in this realm fall quickly into the crystal-rubbing, tarot reading, "hippy" category that is far too easy to dismiss.

But I believe there is a very real need there.

I believe we are hungry for it…but we have no idea where to dine.

We all know that on our deathbed, we'll wish we spent more time with our kids and working in a soup kitchen.

But how do we teach ourselves to FEEL the delight in living that life?

In the end, being a good person — like everything else - is a journey.

It is a daily practice filled with countless interactions and choices. It is filled with endless opportunities to love.

As we learn, we simply say "Yes" more and more often to the choice to spread love.

I Believe

I believe that Heaven is available in every moment.

I believe that the infinite NOW is waiting for us like a surprise party crowd, crouched and eager for our arrival.

I believe there is only one instance – a timeless, spaceless mobius strip event of unfolding.

I believe human consciousness is witness to but a tiny speck on the mobius strip of the cosmos.

I believe that human perception can absorb only a tiny fraction of the vibrations that make up the universe.

I believe that the gift of that minute range of vibrations during that teeny speck of time is still infinitely more than we could ever hope to comprehend or appreciate.

I believe that being conscious to witness ANY of it is a gift beyond measure.

I believe that "awe" is more important than understanding.

I believe that in birth we awaken into a finite consciousness. And in death we rejoin the infinite consciousness.

I believe we can go infinitely microscopic or infinitely telescopic and never find the end of near-miraculous order and harmony.

I believe we wrongly see ourselves as a collection of memories and socialized ideas layered on top of who we really are.

I believe that the interworkings of the cosmos – from atoms to DNA to ecosystems to solar systems to galaxies – are beautiful beyond human comprehension.

I believe that these interworkings of the cosmos have a directional flow towards order, rhythm, and harmony.

I believe that Flow is not something you can understand – but instead must surrender to.

I believe that Flow can be described as Love. Or God.

I believe that Love & Gratitude are the only human truths.

I believe that a human perspective can never have the vantage point to judge ANYthing as good or bad. We can only hope to perceive if we are in or out of alignment with Love.

I believe that each finite consciousness is like a drinking straw being dipped in the cosmic stream. And all of our socialized beliefs are like deposits inside the straw that impede the flow.

I believe that when we get clear and are in alignment with the Flow, then we move through our lives effortlessly – and "God's" will acts through us.

I believe that human consciousness is the universe's way of seeing itself.

I believe that human brains have the ability to transcend the physical realm, yet most humans seek to instead shape the physical realm to meet their desires.

I believe that shaping the physical realm, instead of working with it harmoniously, is a powerful example of being out of alignment.

I believe that this state of being out of alignment is to our consciousness potential as a cancerous cell is to the body.

I believe that surrender is more important than conquest.

I believe that there is no such thing as ordinary or extraordinary.

I believe that infinity can be perceived in the Now.

I believe that the ability to dance, laugh, cry, make love, and watch the sunset should be enough to make everyone feel rich beyond measure.

I believe that there are an infinite number of things to notice in the universe, but a finite number of minutes in a human life – Therefore our choice of focus is critical.

I believe the universe is unfolding according to cosmic DNA present since the big bang.

I believe that in this moment – as you read this – we are connected.

I believe that, long before we ever knew each other existed – we were connected.

I believe that all of my beliefs are simply expressions of understanding in the current moment – and are evolving constantly.

Thank you.

I love you.

Namaste.

dig deeper:

www.LifeStudent.com

www.HugNation.com

www.BeliefBuffet.com

www.1stSaturdays.org

www.Lustmonkey.com

www.PinkHeartCamp.com

www.GrandpaCaleb.com

www.JohnStyn.com

connect:

Facebook.com/JohnStyn

Twitter.com/Halcyon

YouTube.com/HalcyonStyn

Myspace.com/CockyVision

Ustream.tv/channel/HugNation

john@lovemorefearless.com

inspirations:

www.BeliefBuffet.com/recommended

Made in the USA
Lexington, KY
09 May 2014